W9-AXF-173

Emergency Rescue

Angela Royston

Illustrated by
Roger Stewart

Heinemann Interactive Library
Des Plaines, Illinois

Contents

© 1998 Reed Educational & Professional Publishing
Published by Heinemann Interactive Library, an imprint of Reed Educational & Professional Publishing,
1350 East Touhy Avenue, Suite 240 West
Des Plaines, Illinois 60018

Library of Congress Cataloging-in-Publication Data
Royston, Angela.
    Emergency rescue/Angela Royston; illustrated by Roger Stewart.
        p. cm.
    Includes bibliographical references and index.
    Summary: Descibes the work of paramedics, firefighters,
doctors, mechanics, and other emergency rescue workers.
        ISBN 1-57572-173-2 (lib. bdg.)
        1. Rescue work — Juvenile literature. 2. Search and rescue operations — Juvenile literature.
3. Fire extinction — Juvenile literature. 4. Emergency medical services — Juvenile literature.
[1. Rescue work.] I. Stewart, Roger, ill. II. Title.
TL553.R69   1997   97-16132
363.34'8 — dc21   CIP
                                                                                  AC

Photo credits: page 6: Panos Pictures and 23 © D K Hulcher; page 9 and 11: ZEFA; page 12:
© The Automobile Association; page 18: RSPCA Photolibrary © Jonathan Plant; page 20: J Allan Cash Ltd.

Editor: Alyson Jones; Designer: Peter Clayman; Picture Researcher: Liz Eddison
Art Director: Cathy Tincknell; Production Controller: Lorraine Stebbing

Printed and bound in Italy.
See-through pages printed by SMIC, France.

02 01 00 99 98
10 9 8 7 6 5 4 3 2 1

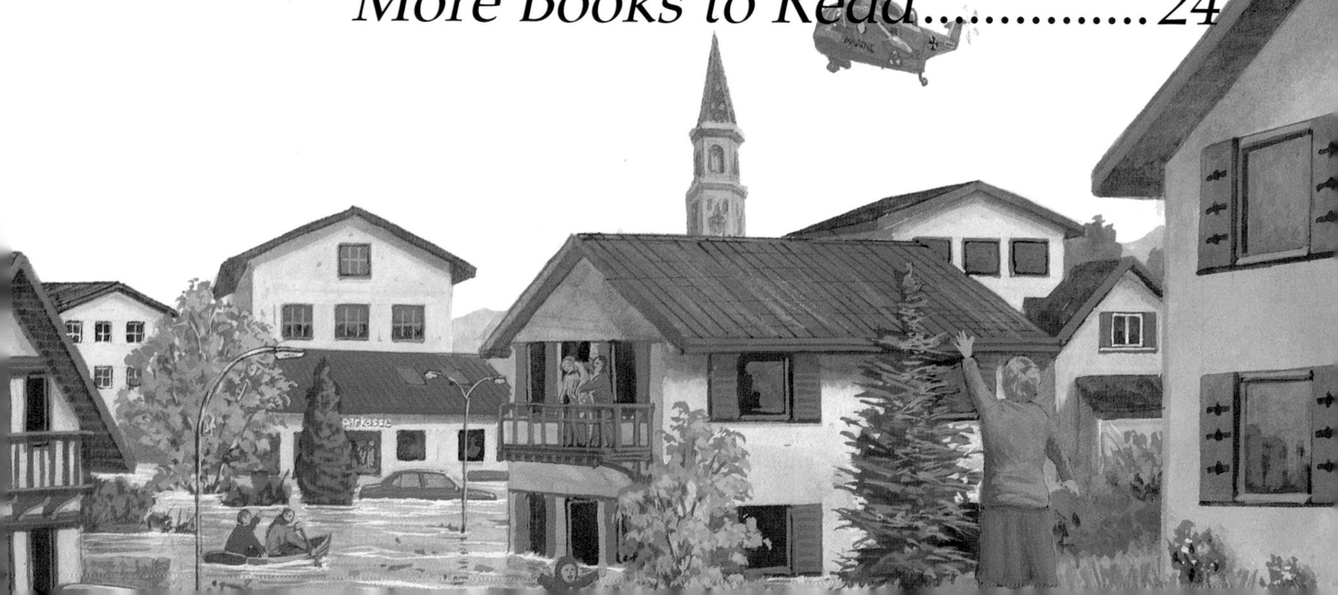

Ready for Action

Rescue workers are always ready to help people who are in danger. Every day they practice their skills and make sure that their vehicles are clean and ready for action.

This is the control room of an ambulance station. The people answer **emergency** telephone calls and tell each ambulance where to go. Help is on the way!

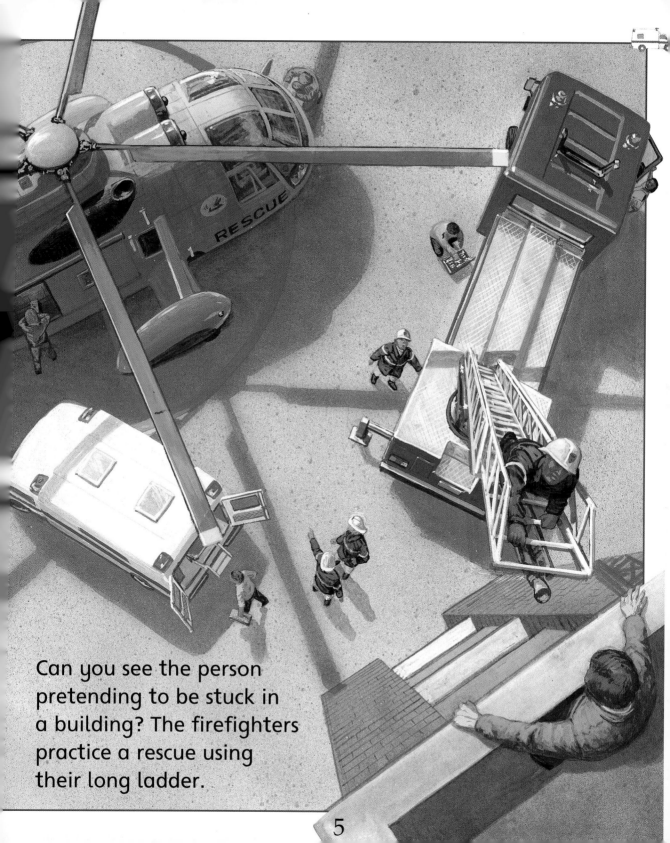

Can you see the person pretending to be stuck in a building? The firefighters practice a rescue using their long ladder.

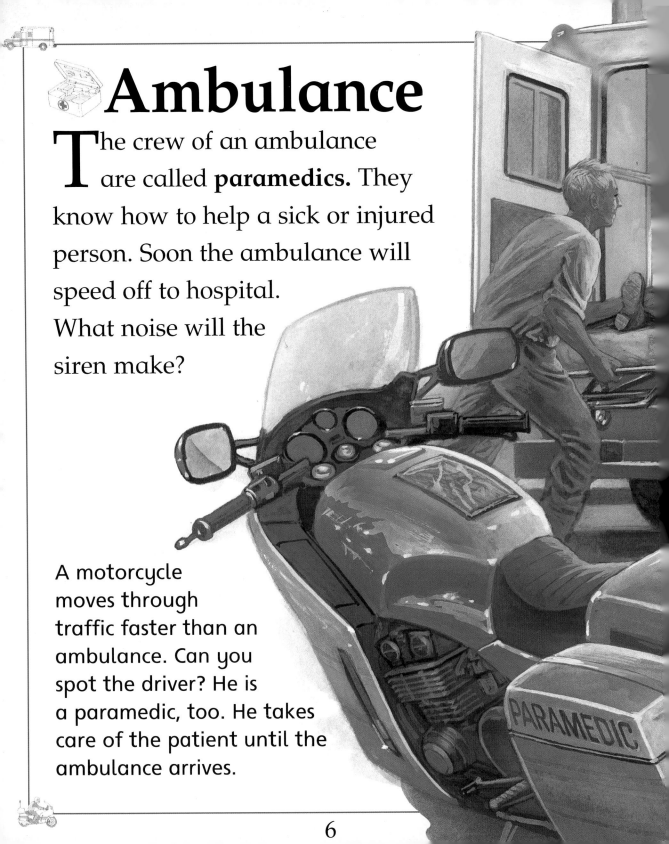

Ambulance

The crew of an ambulance are called **paramedics.** They know how to help a sick or injured person. Soon the ambulance will speed off to hospital. What noise will the siren make?

A motorcycle moves through traffic faster than an ambulance. Can you spot the driver? He is a paramedic, too. He takes care of the patient until the ambulance arrives.

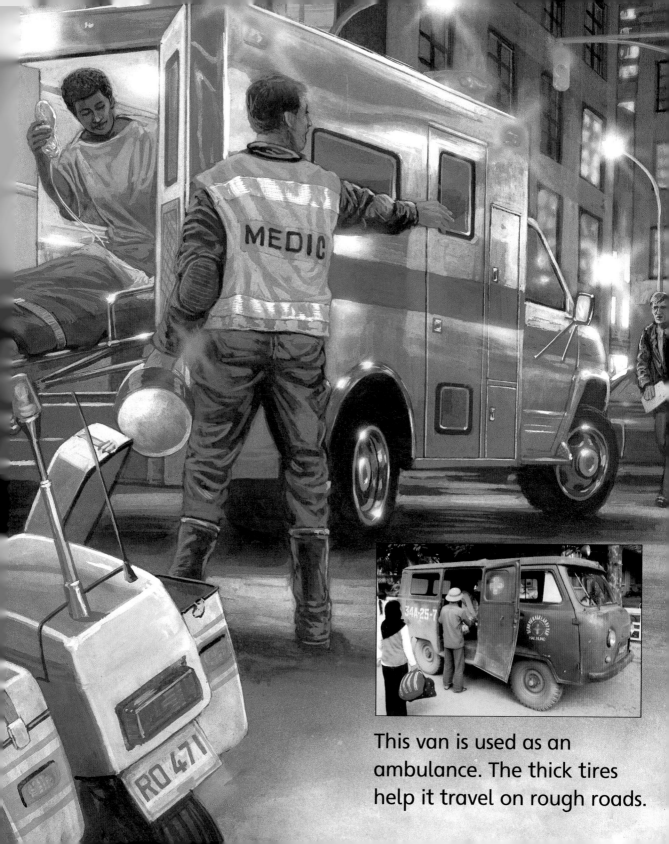

This van is used as an ambulance. The thick tires help it travel on rough roads.

Fire!

A building is burning. Here come some fire engines to put out the blaze. The firefighters unroll the **hoses** and use water from a tank inside the fire engine or from pipes under the ground. They spray water to put the fire out.

Can you see the firefighter connecting a hose to the fire **hydrant?**

This firefighter wears a special suit and mask to protects her from the smoke and heat. She must quickly get away from the flames.

This fire engine has a long ladder. It reaches high up the building.

FIRE DEPT.

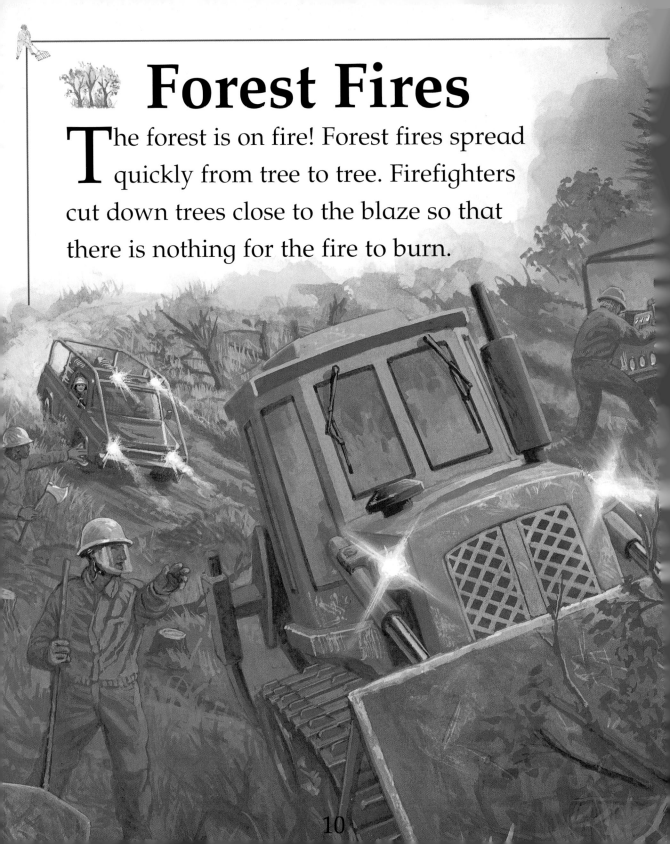

Forest Fires

The forest is on fire! Forest fires spread quickly from tree to tree. Firefighters cut down trees close to the blaze so that there is nothing for the fire to burn.

When there is no water in the forest, the fire trucks bring water in their special tanks.

This helicopter is carrying water. It drops it onto the burning forest beneath to help put out the fire.

⚠ Breakdown

What happens when your car breaks down? A tow truck hauls the car onto the back of the truck. You and your family sit in the cab behind the driver and the truck takes you to a garage.

Some **mechanics** repair cars at the side of the road.

This tow truck lifts up the front wheels of the car. The truck then tows the car to a nearby garage to be repaired.

Flying Doctor

Many **ranches** in Australia are too far from a hospital to go there by road. When this worker had an accident, the farmer radioed for help. The flying doctor has just landed!

This doctor's plane has pontoons as well as wheels so it can land on water. Here it is landing on a lake.

This helicopter has lifted an injured person from a crowded city street. It will reach the hospital faster than the ambulance stuck in traffic below.

Rescue at Sea

Sometimes ships need help. This **oil tanker** has hit the rocks. Can you see the oil spilling into the sea? The **tugs** are trying to pull the oil tanker off the rocks. The orange lifeboat has rescued most of the tanker's crew.

Lifeguards watch out for swimmers who are in danger. They swim out to rescue them. The float keeps the swimmer up while the lifeguard pulls him in.

The storm has gotten worse
and the tanker is beginning
to sink. A helicopter lifts
the rest of the crew off the
oil tanker one by one

Animal Rescue

Animals may need to be rescued, too. If a whale is washed onto the shore, it can breathe but it cannot move. Don't worry! The rescue workers keep the whale cool until it can be floated back to the sea.

Some dogs are dangerous. This dogcatcher has a shield to protect her as she loops a leash around the dog's head.

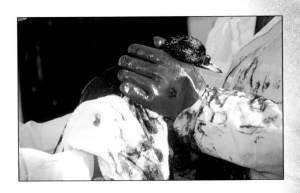

This bird is covered with oil from a wrecked oil tanker. It is held by a rescue worker who will use special soap to clean its feathers.

18

Mountain Rescue

Climbers and skiers sometimes get lost or injured. Can you see which skier has broken her leg? Her friend lights a **flare** to show the helicopter where they are.

Many mountain villages have their own rescue teams. They go on foot to look for people who are lost or injured.

A rescue team has found this injured climber. The team will carry him down to safety on a stretcher.

The climber and the rescue worker are both clipped to the cable. The helicopter hovers as they are lifted to safety.

21

Everyone Helps

A big **disaster** can destroy hundreds of homes. When a river overflows its banks, many people might be stranded. Everyone tries to help each other. Who will rescue the people on the roof?

These workers are unloading food. It will feed people who have lost their homes.

Glossary

Crew Team of people working on a ship or other vehicle.

Disaster Event that causes great damage or injury.

Emergency Something that calls for immediate action.

Flare Kind of large firework.

Hose bendy tube.

Hydrant Special pipe that joins to water pipes under the ground.

Mechanic Person who repairs engines and machines.

Paramedic Person who is trained to do emergency first aid.

Oil tanker Large ship for carrying oil.

Ranches large farms.

Tug Small boat with a powerful engine used for towing larger ships.

Index

More Books To Read

Otfinoske, Steven. *To the Rescue: Firetrucks Then and Now.* Tarrytown, NY: Benchmark, 1997.

Brady, Peter. *Firetrucks.* Mankato, Minn.: Bridgeston, 1996.

Wolhart, Dayna. *Emergency Vehicles.* Mankato, Minn.: Capstone, 1991.